My Sermon Notes

Volume 3

Bishop Kenneth O. Robinson

COMMENTS

"A wonderful book that shows the process of sermon preparation from the initial concept of a subject to a logical outline that can be utilized by Pastors and laymen."

    Bishop Elroy Lewis
    Fischer Memorial UHCA
    Durham, North Carolina
    President, Western No. Carolina District

"Bishop, We often long for material that can inspire and provide a depth of knowledge. The through-ness of your outlines have given me great insight and a broader dimension into the most common scriptures. I trust that you will be encouraged and inspired to continue to bless us thru your giving authorship."

    Superintendent Emory James
    Ephesians New Testament Church
    Fontana, California

"The call and task of preaching will always consume the total being of the Preacher. It is then often expressed through the passion in sermon delivery. In reading the various sermons by Bishop K.O. Robinson, it is amazing to experience that same passion through the written sound doctrinal messages. It is an amazing book of sermons capsulizing a lifetime of successful preaching, inspiring and instructional to any pulpiteer that holds a copy of this timeless book."

    Dr. Aaron B. McNair, Sr.
    New Mt. Moriah Church
    Farmville, North Carolina
    Mt. Moriah Church
    Raleigh, North Carolina

"Bishop Kenneth O. Robinson's book onMy sermon Notes is very informative in its structure, content and outline of the Word of god. It is quietly inspiring in enriching ones spirituality; and it is very thought provoking in motivating one to positive thinking and progressive Christian action. It could be a very useful item to add to ones library."

Bishop John Wright
Holy Temple UHCA
New Haven, Connecticut
President, New England District

"Bishop Robinson, your book cut my research and study time in half on four of my sermons. The book was also a blessing and inspiration to three of my Liberian Pastors. Thank you.

Bishop Raymond S.K. Johnson
Salala Mission Liberia, West Africa

"Bishop Robinson's book is the solution to the lost art of preaching systematic sermon preparation. This book is a vital tool for anyone who is serious about preaching the gospel."

Dr. Kenneth O. Robinson, Jr.
DreamLife Worship Center
Randallstown, Maryland

"Bishop Robinson, your wisdom and knowledge in this book is a great contribution, not only to the United Holy Church, but to the body of Christ."

Bishop Terry McZeke
South Carolina District Convocation

"I perused the book and was pleased with the contents. Those are excellent sermon notes, and they have given me insight on preparation of my sermons. I am a new Elder, and it serves to guide me as I grow. God bless you."

Elder Dorothy James
St. James UHC,
Richmond, Virginia

"My preferred style of preaching is expository. Bishop Robinson has always captured my attention, because he has always remained authentic to his "anointing," i.e preaching sound doctrine. Just prior to his telling me about his book, I said to him and others, Bishop Robinson needs to compile his sermons. This book is a blessing to those looking for a model of remaining true to the text where we can listen to God speaking to us in a relevant way for "holy living." I thank God for for the golden nuggets of inspiration and reflection."

Dr. Lena Thompson, General Chair
Education Department, UHCA, INC.

"Bishop, I am sorry to admit that I have read the book in only portions, in a scanning manner. However, the work is essentially you, reflective of your intensive deductive preaching style, revealing your fervent commitment to scriptural truth and holiness doctrine. I commend you and encourage you to continue your writing activity, especially as it relates to writing. Writing is a valuable vehicle for passing on one's theological insights and legacy. Drive and go forward!

Bishop Clifford Buckhram
Southern District (Henderson)

My
Sermon
Notes
Volume 3

Bishop
Kenneth O. Robinson

inCahoots
LITERARY
Oklahoma City

Published by InCahoots Literary
a division of InCahoots Film Entertainment LLC
Oklahoma City

www.incahootsliterary.com
www.incahootsfilmentertainment.com

Book design and layout by Michael Allen of InCahoots Literary

ISBN 978-0-9887241-9-8

Dedication

This book is lovingly dedicated in memory of the late Bishop Kenneth O. Robinson, former Vice-President of the United Holy Church of America, Inc.

To his amazing bride and wife of 56+ years, Mother Ada Robinson, who stood beside him in all his years of ministry.

To his family; his children, grandchildren and great grandchildren, that he faithfully provided for and served many years.

To the church that he loved and served for 60 years, The United Holy Church of America, Inc.

Contents

Preface

It is with a sense of great joy that I am able to continue with my assignment to publish my sermon notes. I am very much encouraged by the response that my first volume received. Many pastors and ministers have expressed to me how much they were helped in their ministry. Also, many lay-people, who are not ministers, stated that they were highly blessed by the contents of the book. I am thankful to all of you for your support and your gracious comments, some of which you can read in this book.

I believe that you will be equally blessed by Volume 3. It contains more sermons that I have prepared and preached over the many years of my ministry. Some of the sermons were preached during the early years of my ministry and therefore contain less substance. However, they do have structure and a central theme that can be developed with further study and prayer. There are many more sermons in Volume 3 than in the first volume of *My Sermons Notes*.

Many have asked me whether there were any limits on the use of these sermons. Some even felt that they would be guilty of plagiarism or literary theft, if they preached these sermons. Be assured that this would not be the case. You are free to use these notes in any way that the Lord shall direct you, whether you use my name or not. The main objective is to "feed the flock of God."

My prayer is that these sermon notes will be very helpful to you in your ministry and will prove to be a great blessing to you, even if you are not a minister of the gospel.

Acknowledgements

It is truly an honor to continue my father, Bishop Kenneth O. Robinson's legacy. He was a giant of a man, husband, father, pastor and preacher whose life and ministry impacted so many lives.

I can remember it like it was yesterday, when he and I sat down and talked about doing a book of his sermons. I told him that sermon preparation has become a lost art in many pulpits, and that he would help many new generation preachers if he would put his sermon notes in a book.

This book is an extension of his life and legacy. This third volume is very special because it was the last one he would personally type, and his last desire was that we would get it published. Well, here it is, another awesome compilation of some of his best outlines which are ageless because they are so doctrinally sound.

Of course, none of this would be possible without the following people, who were very instrumental in our collaborative effort to get this done, and I want to thank each of them. First, his granddaughter, Janelle Judd, who searched and searched and was able to find these last notes on his computer. Secondly, I want to thank Tracy Isaac, the editor, who did such a wonderful job with editing all the sermon outlines.

Finally, to all of you who support us in the continuance of this legacy by obtaining a copy of this masterful volume series *My Sermon Notes* by the late Bishop Kenneth O. Robinson.

Dr. Kenneth O. Robinson Jr.

References

It would be impossible to list all the sources that I've had access to in preparation of these sermon notes. However, this is a partial list of the resources that I used:

The Thompson Chain Reference Bible

The Scofield Reference Bible

The Amplified Bible

The New Life Study Bible

The Sword of the Lord Ministries

The Books of Herbert Lockyer, Litt. D.

Evidence That Demand a Verdict, Josh M. McDowell

Great Doctrines of the Bible, William Evans

Elemental Theology, Emory H. Bancroft

Vines Expository Dictionary

The African American Pulpit

and a host of others too numerous to mention for which I am extremely grateful.

My
Sermon
Notes
Volume 3

Bishop
Kenneth O. Robinson

The Trouble Maker

Text: I Kings 18:16–24

Introduction:

Elijah did not fit modern conception of a preacher. He was a disturber, an up-setter, and a trouble maker. He evaluated and criticized the times that he lived in.

A. The Occasion of the Test.

>1. Ahab was a wicked King who led Israel into the idolatrous worship of Baal and sought to destroy the worship of Jehovah by killing off the prophets.

>2. Elijah prayed and the heavens were shut up and no rain or dew fell.

>3. He was accused by Ahab of being a trouble maker.

B. This is the cry of all those that resist the truth. This is the reproach that all of God's men bear.

>1. All the prophets.

>>a. Jeremiah.

>>b. Ezekiel, Hosea, and Amos.

>2. John the Baptist – Herod.

>3. Jesus disturbed the hallowed sanctuaries of Pharisees, Herod's throne, and Pilate and his wife.

4. The apostles turned the world upside down. Paul upset whole cities and made the High Priests angry.

C. If you preach the truth and cry out against unrighteousness, you will be a trouble maker.

D. But, this is God's way.

Reservation in Heaven:
Have You Made Your Reservation?

Text: I Peter 1:3–4

Introduction:

A reservation is anything kept back, held in store for future use. It is exclusively and expressively for the one for whom it is reserved. It is kept so by having your name put on it.

A. Everybody is thrilled when we talk about heaven and many entertain thoughts of going there, but have you got a reservation?

B. The idea of reservations should not seem strange. Many places in this life require one.

    1. For convenient.

    2. For purposes of limiting the number.

    3. For prejudice – discrimination.

    4. To give the place an air of exclusiveness; something special.

C. Now heaven is a place of reservation – a prepared place for prepared people.

    1. Not for the trivial reasons man gives.

    2. But, because it has pleased God to prove His faithfulness and to certify the truth of his Word and His promise.

D. Citizenship in heaven is not limited to any particular group, yet you cannot make a reservation yourself.

    1. The only one that can make your reservation is Jesus. John 14:1, 6.

    2. Do you know Him? Has He written your name in His book?

Watchman, What of the Night?

Text: Isaiah 21:11–12

Introduction:

It is getting darker in this evil age and never has it been as dark as it is now. This is the night of God Prophetic Day. All around troubles mount.

A. Worldly Darkness.

> 1. Worldwide major tragedy from which recovery seems impossible. Resources of diplomacy exhausted – inevitable crash awaited.

> 2. Famine – unrest shaky governments.

B. National Confusion – Vietnam War, Inflation, Crime, Wildness of Youth, and Moral Revolution

C. Even in the church world.

> 1. God's word is being rejected, perverted, and distorted until there is a host of doctrines, beliefs, etc. God is dead.

> 2. Our churches are filled with nominal mouth-confessing Christians who sing God's praises on Sunday and go away. Day of the falling away because iniquity is abounding the love of many.

> 3. Only the blind or spiritually ignorant can deny the truth. I can hear the voice of the dissenter.

D. The morning cometh even so for us, God's true church, the church invisible.

    1. The increasing darkness means the approaching of the dawn.

    2. God's Morning – when all saints of God will be gathered home.

E. Four Watches. Mark 13:35.

    1. Sunset for three hours.

    2. Then to midnight.

    3. Then for three hours more.

    4. Then to sunrise.

        a. Christ, the Son of Righteousness appears.

The Gospel According to You, How Do You Read?

Text: II Corinthians 3:3 (1-3)

Introduction:

Paul defends his apostleship to fragmented and divided Corinthian church. False teachers caused them to lose confidence in Paul and to doubt his apostolic authority. Paul defends his apostleship by stating that they were his evidence.

A. Letters of commendation help many times to get advancement in life.

> 1. Nice to have.
>
> 2. But can be deceiving because they can be bought or the result of friendship.

B. Paul sets forth a vital truth of Christianity – that we are epistles of Christ.

> 1. Living Letters commending Christ to the world.
>
> 2. Not only that but we represent Christ. We are the light of the world.
>
> 3. Someone said that Christianity is Christ received, realized, and reproduced.
>
> 4. This is the ideal, but with so many, reality is vastly different..

C. We, as Christians, ought to strive to be like Jesus and let the beauty of Jesus be seen in us because:

1. We are known – not our actual standing before God but our profession of faith.

2. We are read by all men.

D. Everyone that claims to be a Christian has a responsibility to live and act ike a Christian because we are being read.

Spiritual Shipwrecks

Text: I Timothy 1:19 (18–20)

Introduction:

Paul encourages his son in the Gospel – Timothy – to keep the faith and not allow himself to become a spiritual shipwreck. Shipwrecks were a common sight in those days. They were tragic sights.

A. Things to make shipwreck of.

    1. Life – pictured as an ocean.

        a. Having two shores – birth and death.

        b. Our lives as ships upon the sea.

        c. Sin causes our life to become shipwrecked.

    b. Our Christian Faith.

        a. How tragic this is when we push off from the shores of sin heading toward that heavenly city.

        b. But somewhere along the way we are found spiritual-shipwrecks.

        c. How much of this do we have today – shipwreck concerning the faith?

B. What causes shipwrecks?

    1. Little or no preparation.

        a. Dry dock – preparation.

b. Ample supplies or provision.

2. The Journey itself becomes difficult.

   a. Contrary winds begin to blow – rocks – boisterous waves.

   b. In the Christian life, this is also true.

C. How to keep from being shipwrecked.

   1. We need a chart and compass – The Bible.

   2. We need and anchor for the soul – hope.

   3. We need Jesus as our pilot and captain.

What Are You Looking For?

Text: II Peter 3:10–14

Introduction:

Peter warns the people against false teachers and falling away and reminds them of their Christian hope.

A. The Christian life is one of expectation and hope.

    1. Not merely to escape hell.

    2. It is based upon a definite promise made to him by God.

    3. He is looking for something.

B. What are we looking for?

    1. The day of the Lord.

    2. New earth and new heaven.

    3. New body.

    4. Looking for Jesus just to behold His face, "Oh I want to see Him, look upon His face."

C. This Christian expectation governs our whole manner of life.

    1. Our hope is linked to certain conditions.

    2. Or qualifications which must be fulfilled.

    3. We understand that none but the righteous shall see God.

    4. Heaven is a prepared place for a prepared people.

D. Because of these things, we are urged to be diligent.

    1. Our Christian hope urges us to be careful about our actions.

Harps Upon the Willows

Text: Psalms 137:1–6

Introduction:

The lament of the Israelites in the land of Babylon.

A. This is the cry of lost blessings which are the results of disobedience.

    1. No joy in backsliding.

    2. They remembered how things were.

    3. We ought to take advantage of our opportunity to worship and to serve.

B. Harps upon the willows.

    1. Harps are a symbol of talents or gifts.

    2. Upon the willows means talents or gifts that are neglected or put aside.

    3. The church and the world suffer today because men waste or neglect the gift that God gave them.

C. Neglect and misuse ruins the gift or the individual.

D. The Cause

    1. Sin.

    2. Discouragement.

3. Chastening.

4. Disobedience.

5. Retirement.

E. Exhortation is to take your harp off of the willows.

1. Go back and get it again.

2. Right where you left it.

3. Ask God's forgiveness and cleansing.

4. Pray that you may redeem the time by using your God-given talents to the glory of God and for the building up of His Kingdom.

Rejoice in the Lord

Text: Philippians 3:1–4:4

Introduction:

To rejoice means to be glad, to be filled with joy, and this is the command given by God through the apostle. At first thought one might think that in these days and times, it is impossible to fulfill. However, the Bible gives us several reasons that why Christians ought to be happy always.

A. Luke 10:20

> 1. Salvation is reason enough.
>
> 2. Not how the Lord uses us (abilities, achievements, and possessions)
>
> 3. If you are not saved, you have nothing really to rejoice about.

B. Romans 12:12 – rejoicing in hope.

> 1. What is hope? Expectation.
>
> 2. If we really expect to go to heaven and to be with Jesus, then why not be happy.

C. Romans 5:3 – tells us to rejoice in tribulations.

> 1. Do we really do this? We should if we don't.
>
> 2. Tribulations work for our good.

D. When should we rejoice?

    1. Always - not fair weather only

    2. Everywhere – at home and on the job; we should always carry a cheerful, pleasant countenance.

A Stone of Remembrance

Text: I Samuel 7:12

Introduction:

These are the words of Samuel as he erected a stone of memorial to God's divine help and support for a recent victory. The stone was called "Ebenezer," meaning, "stone of help." Every time Israel looked at the stone, they would remember how God had helped them.

A. Stones and Rocks were used for markers and signs …

    1. For example, Abraham (Genesis 12:7), Jacob (Genesis 28:16–22).

    2. This stone was a sign to Israel that God was their divine support.

    3. This stone caused them to look back and remember what God had done.

B. Looking back sometimes can be unwise.

    1. Lot's wife looked back and was turned into a pillar of salt.

    2. Children of Israel looked back and remembered the fleshpots of Egypt.

    3. Jesus warns against looking back after one has started this Christian journey.

C. Every Soul needs their Stone of Ebenezer. That is, they need to remember how God has helped them.

1. You need to remember the pit from which you were drawn.

2. "He brought me up from a horrible pit and out of the miry clay."

3. You need to remember how He guided you through the sifting sands of life, through the wind and the rain, the good and the bad, etc.

4. You need to look back in the Spirit and take courage, trust in His help in times to come.

5. These remembrances are our "Ebenezers," our stones of remembrances.

D. As I look at my "Ebenezer" we can say:

1. As one writer put it, "God has been better to me than I have been to myself, better than all my hopes, greater than all my fears, stronger than all my weaknesses. He turned my griefs into rainbows of glory. He was in the storms that threatened me; I didn't always see Him, but He wrought a mighty deliverance. When I was sad, His presence diminished my sorrows and gave me joy."

2. As we view our Stone of Remember, our Ebenezer, we can sing, "We have come this far by faith, leaning on the Lord."

3. Or we can say, "Through many dangers, toils and snares, I have already come; it was grace that brought me safe thus far, and grace will carry me on."

4. "I will continue to look to the hills from whence cometh my help, my help cometh from the Lord."

Conclusion:

I am glad that I have some stones of remembrances in my life, and when I back at my Ebenezers, I am encouraged "for hitherto, has the Lord helped us."

Let Jesus Lead You

Text: Psalms 48:14, 23:2–3

Introduction:

The uncertainty of the future ought to make us seek the guidance of God.

A. First of all, we need Him to lead us.

　1. You cannot make the journey by yourself.

　2. He promised to lead us and to guide us. I will guide thee with mine eye.

　3. Because of the enemy

B. He is able to lead because He is the Good Shepherd.

　1. A Good Shepherd will lead His sheep. He goeth before them and guides them around the dangers.

　2. This implies of course that we are sheep – humble lambs willing to follow where ever He leads.

C. Let us look at how He leads.

　1. First of all, by His example that He left us.

　2. By His word that he left on record for us to read.

　3. By holy pastors which mean "Shepherd," to counsel, teach, and preach.

　4. By circumstances good and bad.

5. By the Holy Ghost.

D. Where He leads:

    1. Beside still waters.

    2. In the paths of righteousness.

    3. To that heavenly city – New Jerusalem.

What Makes a Man Turn His Back on God

Text: II Timothy 4:10, I Timothy 1:9, 2 Peter 3:17, Hebrews 3:12

Introduction:

The subject today is backsliding. An important one because today is the day of falling away. So much so that many doubt God's power to keep. But God saves to keep, and we are not of those who draw back in perdition.

A. What makes a person "fall away" or turn his back on God?

    1. Is it because God is not good or has not been good?

        a. God says unto Israel, "What iniquity have ye found in me?" – Jeremiah 2:5

        b. Any honest person has to confess that God is good.

    2. Is it because God asks of us that which is not possible?

        a. Can men live holy?

        b. Yes, there is proof in the lives of godly people.

    3. Is it because God has forsaken us?

        a. You have forsaken me – you have gone backwards.

        b. I will be with thee unto the sixth hour – always even unto the end of the world.

    4. We can conclude that the failure is not in God, but in man.

B. What makes a man turn His back on God?

    1. It is possible that they have never been saved?

    2. Do not want to pay the price

    3. Fail to crucify flesh, mortify the members of the body.

    4. Love of the world.

C. There is a plan in God where the soul cries out, "I won't go back. I can't turn my back on God; I'm too close to heaven."

D. How to keep from "Falling away."

The Results of Obedience

Text: John 2:1–5 (I Samuel 15:22)

Introduction:

We live in a day when there is a general disregard of authority or rules, or regulations of any kind. The revolt of our young people is mainly a revolt against authority. Religion is rejected; even within the church, people feel free to obey or not obey as they see fit.

A. A spirit of disobedience:

B. The dynamics of obedience.

    1. Humility, pride manifests itself in disobedience.

    2. Faith – confidence inspires obedience.

    3. Submission to higher power – recognition that there is a power higher than self.

    4. Love not always present, but certainly will produce, when present, the greatest degree of obedience.

C. Christian Obedience includes:

    1. Obeying God – supreme.

    2. Obey His voice.

    3. Obey His Ministers.

    4. Some twist the order of priority.

D. The importance of obedience.

    1. Disobedience was the original sin.

    2. God now says unto man – hear and your soul shall live.

        a. Israel was commanded to obey God's commandments – Deuteronomy 26:16.

        b. Their obedience secured for them special status and blessings – Exodus 19:5.

        c. Jesus exalts obedience to Him and His words as the means of membership in his family. Divine security is the key to spiritual knowledge. This is the primary evidence of your love for Him.

A Clean Conscience

Text: Acts 24:16, Proverbs 20:27

Introduction:

The Bible has a good deal to say about conscience. For God works through conscience to bring us to repentance, to cause us to judge ourselves; and if we fail to repent, in hell, conscience will be our greatest tormentor.

A. What is conscience?

    1. Knowing of oneself.

        a. Man's distinguishing feature.

        b. A principle of reflection in many by which he distinguishes between right and wrong.

        c. A moral impeccable "I ought" which troubles us.

    2. A faculty or power implanted by God in every man – sinners – Romans 2:14–16.

        a. The voice of God

        b. The call of God proving that all men could be saved.

        c. But, men resist the call of conscience and resist when conscience is awakened – Stephen.

        d. But, resisting causes the conscience to become defiled and deadened.

3. The conscience does need to be eradicated, but should never be resisted for it speaks for God.

4. How important, then, to have a clear conscience.

    a. For soul peace.

    b. Assurance of eternal life

    c. Assurance that your prayers are answered.

    d. A good relationship with your brother or sister in Christ.

    e. full and continuing joy.

All Sufficient Grace:
My Grace is Sufficient

Text: II Corinthians 12:6–10 (vs. 9)

Introduction:

Paul explains how "Thorn in the flesh" was given to keep him from being exalted.

A. Paul's Thorn

  1. Believed to be physical infirmity – eye disease.

  2. Caused him to look loathsome and have speech contemptible.

  3. None of this can be substantiated in order that we may all benefit from Paul's consolation.

B. We all have our thorn in the flesh. or thorns or cross.

  1. The Christian life is not all smooth sailing.

  2. Sometimes under the load of the cross, we wonder can we make it.

C. Then the words of our text come as comforting.

D. Let us examine the grace of God – definition.

  1. Past.

  2. Present.

  3. Future.

E. Definitions:

    1. Unmerited favor.

    2. The action of God towards us without respect to our deserts.

    3. It is demonstrated in:

        a. Our election and predestination.

        b. Our calling.

        c. Our redemption and justification through Christ – Romans 3:23.

        d. His power and strength for the journey.

    4. Sufficient for every need.

Seek the Lord

Text: Hosea 10:12, Psalms 105:4, Amos 8:12, Job 8:5, Daniel 9:3, Psalms 34:10, Zephaniah 2:3, Psalms 22:26, Psalms 69:32 (vs. 10:12 Hosea)

Introduction:

Seeking the Lord is the continuous duty of the Christian. We often exhort the sinner to seek the Lord, and this is alright, but the sinner is first prodded by the Holy Spirit to seek and of himself can do no seeking.

A. The Sinner.

> 1. Feels the need through the work of the Spirit.

> 2. Calls upon God sincerely repenting of his sin.

> 3. Finds God by faith.

B. The majority of text in the Bible concerning seeking God are directed to the people of God.

> 1. The greatest mistake of Christian people is to cease from seeking God.

> 2. This leads to all other sins and evils – slothfulness, indifference, coldness, worldliness, sin.

> 3. Seeking the Lord as a continual activity will sustain one in the Christian life.

C. The Christian seeks God because:

    1. He cannot maintain the Christian life of his himself.

    2. He is commanded to be strong in the power of God.

    3. He needs to know the will of God that he may please Him.

    4. He needs knowledge of God that he may lead others to God.

    5. He needs God's healing and forgiveness.

D. The Christian seeks God through:

    1. His word – Psalms 119:45–94.

    2. By prayer – Job 8:5, Daniel 9:3.

    3. In His House – Deuteronomy 12:5.

E. This is both a collective and individual exercise.

    1. Every Christian must set himself to seek the Lord for his own individual blessings.

    2. Then, there must be the collective enterprise of the church as a whole to seek from God the blessings that God desires to give His people.

F. Finally, there is a promise connect with seeking God.

    1. Not in vain – Isaiah 45:19.

    2. I shall be found – Jeremiah 29:14.

    3. He will give joy – Psalm 22:26.

    4. He will bless with life – Psalm 69:32.

Let Us Go On

Text: Hebrews 6:1

Introduction:

The book of Hebrews was written to Christian Jews who were persecuted because of their faith. As a result of this, some were ready to go back to Judaism.

A. Alternatives.

    1. Going Back.

    2. Going Up.

B. But, Let Us Go On.

    1. Perfection – that is spiritual maturity.

    2. Let us leave the lowlands of spiritual weakness.

C. Let us go on to a more perfect faith – "Without faith it is impossible to please God."

    1. Let us go on to a more perfect love.

D. Let us go on to a higher height and a deeper depth.

    1. New Converts

    2. All the Saints

E. Let us go on because we have nothing to gain by going back.

F. Let us go on even though the way seems hard and the cross seems heavy.

G. Let us go on to that heavenly Canaan land.

Woe, Unto Them That Are At Ease in Zion

Text: Amos 6:1, Psalms 123:4

Introduction:

There is one sin that we, the people of God, must be ever on guard against. That is the sin of indifference. That feeling or lack of feeling for God's house and His program; a feeling of complacency.

A. Among the Jews a common cause of their backsliding.

    1. Amos 6:1.

    2. Isaiah 47:8.

    3. Numbers 32:6.

    4. Joshua 18:3.

    5. II Corinthians 24:5.

B. In today's church we must be careful – the same malady affects us.

    1. Some signs of it.

        a. Matthew 25:43 – lack of concern for the sick and those in trouble.

        b. Half-heartedness – doing some of what we are supposed to do, but not all.

            i. 2 Kings 13:18.

       iii. 2 Chronicles 25:2.

       iv. Jeremiah 3:10.

C. Prayerlessness.

    1. Isaiah 43:22

    2. Isaiah 64:7

    3. Lack of Zeal

D. God help us to become stirred until we shake ourselves and say, "I must be about my Father's business."

    1. For the sake of those who are lost.

    2. For Zion's sake.

The Winners and Losers

Text: II Corinthians 2:14

Introduction:

Words of the Apostle Paul telling how God caused him to be a winner. Everybody wants to be a winner; however, many are not. We want to talk about a particular type of winner. Not as the world considers winners, but a winner in the sense that we all can be winners. When we think of winning and losing, we think of playing a game in a sense.

A. Life is a game.

    1. Two opponents.

    2. Each trying to win and defeat the other.

    3. So is life – so many things trying to defeat and get us from being winners. and so many lose.

B. But in Christ, we can be winners.

    1. Because He was a winner.

        a. Won the battle of temptation.

        b. Won against His enemies.

        c. Won against death.

    2. Because He won, we can win.

        a. Against sin – no more dominion.

        b. Against temptation – a way of escape.

c. Against your enemies.

d. Against death – we will be winners.

C. But our winning is dependent upon whether we are in Christ.

1. Not due to our strength, wisdom, or natural ability.

2. But, our position – as being in Christ – without Him, we are losers.

Divine Reputation

Text: Matthew 16:13–16, Proverbs 22:1

Introduction:

A good reputation is a valuable asset in life. All companies or organizations strive to maintain a good reputation. /we do not want to talk about merely a good reputation.

A. Jesus did not ask because He didn't know who He was:

> 1. But, because He wanted man's opinion – public reaction, not private (vice versa).

> 2. Character is what you are; reputation is what men say you are.

> 3. A divine reputation is based upon a divine character.

B. We, as Christians, ought to be concerned about our divine reputation.

> 1. We ought to know what we are.

> 2. But we ought to be concerned that someone knows it.

> 3. Also our fellow Christians.

C. The Christian community suffers today because everyone that calls themselves does not have a divine reputation.

D. Also, it is a hindrance to the progress of the church.

E. We ought to – all of us – try to acquire and maintain a reputation.

The Evidence of a Grateful Heart:
I am So Grateful

Text: Psalm 116: 1–2, 12–14

Introduction:

Thanksgiving is a season of hypocrisy for men who do not love God as they profess they do. Love carries a sign, and it gives unmistakable evidence of its presence.

A. Men need a reason to really love the Lord.

    1. It is not their natural emotion towards God.

    2. Even merely preaching and teaching about the goodness of God will not make men love God.

    3. But men began to love God when they experienced salvation – the psalmist.

        a. God is gracious.

        b. God is merciful.

B. This love produces evidence that springs forth from a grateful heart.

    1. What shall I render?

    2. What can I do?

C. The Psalmist says he will:

    1. Take the cup of salvation.

    2. Call upon the name of the Lord.

3. Walk before the Lord.

4. Pay my vows.

5. Offer sacrifice of praise.

Too Late

Text: Jeremiah 8:20

Introduction:

The people of God besieged by the Babylonians through a long, hot, dry summer, prayed for deliverance, but none came.

A. This was God's judgment for sin – (vs. 5–7).

    1. God is a god of justice.

    2. He had grown weary with their backsliding.

B. Note the tragic, sad tone of the text.

C. The text teaches of a specific time of opportunity.

    1. Summertime – Life.

    2. Harvest.

D. God's Harvest Time is:

    1. Anytime the Word is preached.

    2. Others are getting saved – Spirit speaks.

E. End of the Harvest.

    1. Death.

    2. When the Spirit ceases to strive.

"We are not saved." How many millions of souls will enter eternity uttering these tragic words? I missed my chance, and now it is too late.

The Power of the Human Will: Ye Will Not Come

Text: John 5:40, 8:24, 21

Introduction:

Some of the saddest words spoken by Jesus ever. The words of a rejected Savior to stubborn willful sinners who chose to remain in sin rather than follow Him. Man is created with a three-fold nature – body, soul, and spirit or emotions, intellect, and will. True conversion involves all aspects of man's composition.

A. Intellect – the power to reason and understand.

B. Emotions – the power to feel.

C. Will – the power to act morally and responsibly. Most causes of failure to experience and receive the grace of God lie in the will – which God has put in our power to exercise.

> 1. Spoken to religious men, their refusal not due to:
>
>> a. Ignorance.
>>
>> b. Intellect.
>>
>> c. But to will
>
> .2. How true today that men do not come to Christ not because of:
>
>> a. Ignorance.
>>
>> b. Intellectual difficulty.

c. Or any inability whatsoever, but simply because they do not want to come.

3. Because:

   a. They love their sin more than God – II Thessalonians 2:12.

   b. They misrepresent the love of God.

4. Jesus said:

   a. If you will not come, you will die.

   b. Ye cannot come where I am going

Consider Your Ways

Text: Haggai 1:3:11

Introduction:

A time of Divine displeasure with the remnant in Israel. God invites them to take a look at themselves and consider their ways. Many times, we are not doing as good as we should be doing and are not as blessed as we could or should be. We ought to consider our ways.

A. Your ways.

    1. Your behavior.

    2. Your attitude.

    3. Every way we have sometime is not Christ-like.

B. Your ways

    1. Not other people's ways.

    2. Fault-finding is uncalled for, and destructive criticism is the mark of a heart that is void of love.

C. Consider:

    1. Means to examine them in the light of God's word, not to justify them.

    2. Means to mend your ways – Jeremiah 7:3–5.

D. The importance of considering your ways.

1. Because people judge you by your ways.

2. Your ways can cause someone to stumble.

3. Your ways can cause even your good to be evil spoken of.

4. Your ways can cause you to go to hell. "There is a way that seemeth right, but the end thereof is death."

The Lesson of Death

Text: Psalm 90:12

Introduction:

In the most solemn occasion, we consider and reflect upon death. The most serious and heart-rendering time of life. Death is never for naught – if we reflect upon it, there is much to be considered. There are always at least two aspects to every death, both a natural and a spiritual.

A. Natural Aspect.

    1. The man or woman who dies – who he was and what he was.

    2. We memorialize him because he died that we might live in the service of his country.

    3. We memorialize him because he has made a supreme sacrifice for his country – his wife, children, and family also share in that sacrifice.

    4. We pray for a day when there will be no need of armies and war, but we realize that as long as there are sinful men wars will be inevitable.

B. Spiritual Aspect.

    1. Death is the greatest lesson that God gives in teaching us to value life.

2. A debt we all must pay. We should consider it at all times. Not that we must live, but that we must die. It cannot be prevented – are you ready?

A Bad Bargain

Text: Matthew 16:25–26

Introduction:

Nobody likes to be cheated. We are very careful to receive from any exchange – full value. But in spiritual matters, many make a bad bargain.

A. What is the Soul?

    1. Man is a Trinity.

        a. Body.

        b. Soul.

        c. Spirit.

    2. Jesus said fear not for the body.

    3. Soul – self consciousness – the real you.

    4. Body – instrument of the soul.

B. Many questions arise:

    1. But remember the soul as spiritual.

    2. It is eternal – mere physical death of the body does not destroy the soul.

    3. Therefore, we can see the value of the soul over anything temporal.

C. What does it mean to lose one's soul?

    1. Let's take a look at the first time man bargained with his soul.

        a. Adam in the garden.

        b. He experienced:

            i. Physical death.

            ii. Spiritual death.

            iii. Eternal death.

    2. Man today is a lost soul – he is subject to physical death, he is experiencing spiritual death, but he has a chance to escape eternal death.

D. But in the marketplace of life, many bargain away their souls.

    1.Saul, Judas, Demas, Ananais, and Sapphira.

    2. There is nothing in life worth the loss of one's soul.

Another Way

Text: Luke 8:38–39

Introduction:

One of the most remarkable facts about the Christian religion is its ability to change men. No one who has ever come in contact with Jesus has ever been the same.

A. The Man.

    1. Possibly Jesus' worst case.

    2. Demon possessed – completely controlled by the Devil.

    3. What a picture of sinful man at his worst state – out of his mind and naked before God, dwelling in the wilderness, crying leave me alone.

B. What Jesus did.

    1. He rebuked the demons that bound the man's soul.

    2. Gave him a new mind – put clothes on him.

    3. Then sent him home – witnessing.

C. Jesus can send you home today another way.

    1. In sin, you don't have your right mind.

        a. Naked before God.

    2. If you're burdened, troubled, sick, and discouraged, he can send you home another way.

    3. Reason I know is because one day when I was in sin, weary and undone, he sent me home.

D. Have we lost our belief in God's ability to change men?

Let Jesus Fix It For You

Text: Matthew 9:27–35

Introduction:

Life is full of problems – everybody has one. It may not seem like much to another one, but if it bothers you or hinders you, it is a problem.

A. Types of Problems.

    1. World – war, famine, racial.

    2. Church.

    3. Personal Problems.

        a. Sickness.

        b. Financial.

        c. Domestic.

    4. Sin – man's greatest problem.

B. All Types of Ways to Deal with Problems.

    1. V.N. – governmen.t

    1. Doctors, psychiatries, and courts.

    3. Human reasoning and meddling.

    4. No way to deal with sin.

C. Jesus the great problem fixer.

    1. All during His earthly ministry men and women brought their problems to Jesus.

    2. He proved that He could fix all problems. Nothing was too difficult for Him, not even death.

    3. He fixed the biggest problem of all when He died for the sins of the world.

D. Our trouble is that we do not believe that he can do it – (vs. 28).

Jesus is a Friend of Mine: What a Friend We Have in Jesus

Text: John 15:13–15

Introduction:

What a blessing it is to have a friend. We have many acquaintance and associates, but not many friends. A true friend is more precious than fine gold, than money in the bank.

A. What is a friend?

> 1. Webster says, "one attached to another by affection, regard, esteem; an intimate acquaintance; a supporter."
>
> 2. The Bible says in Proverbs 17:17, "a loveth at all times."
>
> 3. Also, Proverbs 18:24 a friend who sticketh closer than a brother.
>
> 4. A confidant – you confide in him and tell him all your secrets, and he will not repeat them.
>
> 5. A friend in need is a friend indeed. A true friend will help you.

B. What a friend we have in Jesus.

> 1. An earthly friend can many times fulfill many of these qualifications of true friendship, but there is only one tried and true friend.
>
> 2. First of all, He loves us:
>
>> a. He proved it on Calvary.

b. Loveth at all times – up and down, in and out, fair-weathered and foul.

c. Intimate acquaintance and confidant. Just tell Jesus; tell Him all.

d. A friend in need steps right in just when I need Him most.

e. My supporter.

C. What a Friend.

1. Sinner – woman caught in adultery – thief on the loose.

2. Sick, blind, and lame.

Progressive or Incomplete Deliverance: The Value of a Second Touch

Text: Mark 8:22–25

Introduction:

Our churches today are filled with people who have been touched by God, but not completely delivered. Incomplete means – unfinished, not half-saved but in the process of being delivered.

A. The man was blind.

    1. Typifies a sinner who is in spiritual darkness.

    2. He was brought to the right man – Jesus.

B. Jesus prayed and the man received partial deliverance.

    1. First, the man did receive a touch.

    2. But it was not a complete deliverance.

    3. It was not that his power was not sufficient to effect a complete deliverance. One touch can heal.

    4. But there is an object lesson here.

C. Jesus would have us to know that sometimes we need more than a touch to be completely delivered – progressive deliverance.

    1. So many people get just a touch, but not complete deliverance.

    2. It is hard to live holy when you are only partly delivered.

D. What is the answer to incomplete deliverance?

1. Jesus prayed again.

2. So many people need to pray again – go back to the altar and call upon the name of the Lord until He completely delivers your soul.

3. Here can be seen the value of the altar and how continual coming. We should ask the Lord to touch us again and again until we are satisfied.

There is a Balm in Gilead

Text: Jeremiah 8:22, 46:11

Introduction:

Jeremiah was concerned over his people's sins. We live in a marvelous age when modern medicine has conquered many of man's diseases, such as malaria, tuberculosis, measles, polio, and there's even some progress on cancer. Many millions are being spent in research with a hope that many more shall be conquered.

A. Sin is a disease of the soul – no cure, vaccine, serum, pill, powder, spray, salve can cure it (Jeremiah 46:11).

    1. It is the worst of all man's disease.

        a. Universal.

        b. Hereditary.

        c. Eternally damaging.

    2. It causes more damage to human life.

    3. It is the root cause of all man's troubles.

B. Jeremiah recognized that the trouble with his people was the disease of sin.

    1. There was a medicine in his day that come from Gilead that was famous for its healing properties. It was so valuable that it was sold for twice its weight in silver.

2. There were those in Gilead who were experts in the use of this balm.

3. But this balm could not save Jeremiah's people.

C. God has a spiritual Gilead (The Church) and there is a balm there that can heal a sin-sick soul.

1. It is the gospel – that is the blood of Christ.

2. It must be applied.

3. It is free for all.

4. We have living proof that it works.

The Way of Holiness

Text: Isaiah 35:8

Introduction:

In these days of false doctrine, false prophets, and confusion, we need the assurance of the Word that we are in the right way – define holiness.

A. God is a Holy God.

    1. His name is Holy – Isaiah 57:15.

    2. His character – Psalm 22:3.

    3. His works – Psalm 145:17.

B. The Bible is a Holy Book.

    1. The Word of God.

    2. Written by holy men moved by the Holy Ghost.

C. His People are a Holy People.

    1. Israel was commanded to be Holy.

    2. God's people today are a Holy People – I Peter 1:15–16.

D. God's people have a:

    1. Holy calling – 2 Timothy 1:9.

    2. Holy walk – I Peter 1:15.

3. Holy home – heaven is a holy place – Revelation 21:27, 22:14–15, Galatians 5:19–21.

E. Application:

1. How we get in the way.

2. How we act while in the way.

3. Where the way leads to.

Good News

Text: Romans 10:15–17

Introduction:

It used to be said that everybody wants to hear good news, but it seems as though bad news is more popular. We need to hear today Good News, talking about:

A. The Gospel.

    1. Defined many ways (the Word of God, truth of God, Jesus Christ, the Blood).

    2. But one of the best definitions is Good News – glad tidings of good things.

    3. The angels so declare it to be so – birth of Christ.

B. The Gospel is Good News because:

    1. The Gospel of peace.

        a. Man and God.

        b. Man.

    2. Glad tiding of good things.

        a. Salvation – Jesus saves.

        b. Healing – by His stripes.

        c. Glorification of saints.

        d. Heaven – home of the redeemed.

e. Wicked shall cease from troubling – "weeping endures for a night, but joy comes in the morning."

3. Good News even when it hurts, rebukes, and corrects.

C. But to some, it is not Good News, but bad news.

1. Tells of judgment, hell, and eternal separation from God.

2. Only to those that believe is it good news – Romans 1:16, 10:16.

What is Saving Faith?

Text: Acts 16:27–34

Introduction:

The Philippians' jailor who is brought fact to face with the power of God asks one of life's most important questions. The answer is a simple one, but widely misunderstood. What does it mean to believe on the Lord Jesus Christ?

A. Believe – Faith.

　　1. The Bible teaches salvation by faith.

　　2. No one has ever been saved that did not exercise faith.

　　3. Acceptance of that not fully known or seen.

　　4. But what must we believe?

　　5. Confidence in that which was done even though you didn't see it.

B. Acting with knowledge or assurance of that which is to come as though it were already here.

　　1. Faith must have a proposed object.

　　2. Believe on me as the scripture has said.

　　3. Not a creed, but a person.

C. We must believe the:

  1.Bible – the Word of God.

  2. Christ – not the historical Christ or the teacher of good morals – the Son from heaven.

  3. The reality of sin.

  4. Our lost condition.

  5. The reality of heaven and hell.

D. Saving Faith is:

  1. Accepting the Living Christ into our heart.

  2. This begins the miracle of regeneration – the receiving of new life supernaturally.

  3. Exercising saving faith will mean a change in character, personality, and life.

Working Together With God and One Another

Text: I Corinthians 3:9

Introduction:

Paul's message to the Corinthian Church – corrupt and divided. He gives strong teaching against sinful practices and attempts to unify the church in the service of God. He presents many cardinal truths which are vital to us today. Truths which Satan many times would have us ignore. Let us consider the text and several key words in it.

A. We.

> 1. Not just the Pastor – he is not the whole church. The key person – the inspiration, encourager, exhorter, chief planner, but not the whole show.

> 2. "We" involves more than just one. In this case, it involves all that are in the church – deacons, trustees, choir members, etc. No one is excluded; all are important.

> 3. We should never individualize any job or program, but the main pronouns should be we, us, and our. When the Lord gives anyone a plan or program – when it is put into operation – it is no more his or hers, but ours.

B. Are - indicates present tense; now – right now. We ought to be working; we cannot rest upon past labors, and we can't be overly dependent upon the future, but right now we need workers.

C. Workers – action people.

    1. Action in pursuit of a goal – we call it a goal.

    2. A real worker produces – productivity is the main thing, but not in the worldly industry.

    3. God calls us from sin and shame and spiritual inactivity to righteousness, purity, and action in His vineyard.

D. Together – implies unity of purpose and coordination of effort, mutual concern, appreciation of the yoke and concept of church work. This means subordination of one's own ideas and submission to the ideas of others even if you do not totally agree or have a better way.

E. With – we are not alone or without help in our labors. We have an unseen partner. We are not the sole owners or masters of the work.

    1. We have a master who is head of the vineyard. He is who commissioned us, hired us, and told us to go into His vineyard and work.

    2. So in a larger sense, the program is not our program, but His.

F. God – our unseen partner and co-laborer.

    1. He supplies the motive, that we might please Him, to do His will and exhibit his love.

    2. The incentive – the rewards of your labor.

    3. To Him, we will make our final report.

    4. From Him, we will receive our highest commendation – Well Done.

The Believers' Rest

Text: Hebrew 4:9

Introduction:

Paul encourages Jewish Christians who were under great stress to continue fighting the good fight of faith because there was a rest awaiting them. Different types of rest are soul rest – freedom from sin.

A. The Jews in the early history are a type of the Christian experience.

> 1. Egypt – type of sin.
>
> 2. Wilderness – type of Christian life here on earth. They had to:
>
> > a. Exercise faith.
> >
> > b. Pray.
> >
> > c. Fight many enemies.
> >
> > d. They were sustained by God – He fed and clothed them.
>
> 3. Canaan, land flowing with milk and honey where the trials of the wilderness would be no more.
>
> 4. Because of unbelief, many did not enter in.

B. Canaan – a type of the believer's rest – typifies heaven.

1. As in Canaan where the work of faith stopped, so in heaven the believers will have to exercise faith no longer.

2. The work of prayer will stop.

3. No more enemies or giants in the land,

4. There will be rest from:

    a. Temptation.

    b. Trials.

    c. Tears.

Molded by His Grace

Text: I Corinthians 15:8–10 (vs.10)

Introduction:

I think that one of the most beautiful words in the English language is the word Grace. When we consider its meaning, our hearts are filled with joy. Then I like to think about what grace has done for me and to me.

A. What is Grace?

> 1. An illustration from life insurance – grace period.
>
> 2. The core of its meaning is receiving or having something done for us that we don't deserve.
>
> 3. In theological language, we say, "the unmerited favor of God toward man."
>
> 4. One writer says, "Everything for nothing to those who deserve nothing."

B. Apostle Paul – a beautiful illustration of the Grace of God.

C. Chosen by grace – Romans 11:5 (a. remnant according to the election of grace.)

D. Called by grace – Galatians 1:15

E. By grace ye are saved.

F. And Grace is molding us right now.

G. Grace woke me up this morning – started me on my way.

H. Grace is keeping me right now.

    1. Through many dangers

    2. Makes me love my enemies

I. Grace enables us to work.

J. And, if we make it to the Glory Land, it will be God's grace that takes us there

The Living God or the God of the Bible – God Is

Text: Hebrews 11:6

Introduction:

Our subject today to many may seem unnecessary, but many people do not believe in the God of the Bible. And as the Bible is rejected, our society is becoming more and more atheistic.

A. Man needs to believe in something greater than himself.

B. Because there is much in life that he cannot understand or explain – nature, universe, and life.

C. But, he refuses to accept the God of the Bible. This is the basic of the God is Dead Theology.

D. He substitutes instead a belief in:

    1. A supreme power.

    2. Polytheism – many gods.

    3. Deism – an impersonal being.

    4. He makes a God out of:

        a. Money.

        b. The status quo.

        c. Sex.

E. All of these have failed him for they do not give him the security, joy, or peace that he seeks, therefore many have concluded that there is not God.

    1. British philosophers

    2. Soviet Cosmonaut

F. If men are ever to find God, they must return to the Bible.

G. Must believe that God is – accepting the reality of his existence as a matter of faith.

H. The Bible does not attempt to prove his existence.

I. God is and God does.

J. He is a person – active in the affairs of men and the universals. He created. He saves. He delivers. He blesses. He cares.

Sing Unto Him a New Song

Text: Psalms 33:1–3, Ephesians 5:19, Colossians 3:16, Psalm 40:3

Introduction:

Thank God for the beauty of singing. Singing is a form of expression that speaks more eloquently sometime, more plainly than ordinary speech or slogans. I love to sing and I enjoy good singing. I believe God loves it.

A. This can be seen.

B. In heaven – ⅓ of which was a choir.

C. Jubal – father of musical instruments

D. God's people the Jews have always been a musical – singing people.

    1. Danced and sang at the Red Sea.

    2. David – the sweet psalmist of Israel.

    3. Sang on the way to Jerusalem.

E. Then God puts into the heart of the redeemed a new song.

F. It is mark of true salvation.

G. It is a new song – a melody the world knows not of.

H. It is a song that keeps ringing in your heart – test, trials, dark of night does not remove the song from your heart. Paul and Silas.

I. Then, we are admonished by Paul to sing and make melody in our hearts unto God.

J. And of course, there will be singing in heaven.

K. The Angels sing God's praises and all of heaven's host.

L. Bu, the redeemed will sing a new song.

Surely This Thing is Known

Text: Exodus 2:11–14, Numbers 32:23

Introduction:

Many people today think that they can sin and get by, and as long as their sin is not known, then it's alright. Therefore, they attempt to hide their sin and continue on as if nothing has happened; but sin can never be concealed.

A. Moses' sin.

    1. He tried to hide it.

    2. But he found out that the sin was not covered.

B. People today are like Moses.

    1. Sin is shameful and condemning and brings the wrath of God and man.

    2. So man uses various ways to conceal his sin.

        a. Adam and Eve – fig leaves.

        b. Achan – hid the wedge in the ground of his tent.

        c. Saul hid behind a testimony – a lot of folks are like this.

        d. David used deceit and the powers of his office. Herod did the same thing.

        e. Ananais and Sapphira lied – the most common.

C. But in every case, they found out – as Moses did – that surely this thing is known and that their sin found them out.

    1. It will find you out.

        a. No matter who you are.

        b.No matter what you are.

        c. No matter where you are.

        d. No matter how long it takes.

    2. It will find you out.

        a. Because God is still on the Throne.

        b. Because we must all stand the test in judgment of Christ and the White Throne.

D. If we are trying to hide sin, we ought to realize, like Moses, that surely this thing is known.

    1, Confession.

    2. Repentance ought to follow this awakening.

The Signs of the Time

Text: Matthew 24:1–3

Introduction:

Jesus' disciples asked three important question concerning judgment, His Coming, and the end of the world. Jesus gave us some signs that would point to these things.

A. Sign – given to identify information, instruction, and guidance.

    1. Must be read and understood.

    2. If you misread the sign, you get lost, are led astray, and become discouraged.

B. Signs to be read.

    1. Signs are peculiar to the world.

        a. Perilous times – II Timothy 3:1.

        b. The war sign.

        c. Great wealth.

        d. Famines – vs.7.

        e. Fig tree sign.

        f. Distress and fear – Leviticus 21:24–27.

        g. Noahic sign, eating, drinking, marrying – 24:37:39.

        h. Increase of knowledge – Daniel 12:4.

2. Church Signs.

    a. Apostasy – II Thessalonians 2:3.

    b. Pleasure sign.

    c. Professional sign denying the power.

    d. Laodicean church sign – Revelation 3:14–22.

C. Signs must be fulfilled, but don't let them be fulfilled in you.

Working for Unity

Text: Ephesians 4:1–3 (vs.3), I Corinthians 1:10

Introduction:

What is unity? Webster says, "it is the state of being one, oneness, harmony, and agreement. Certainly the church ought to have unity. Jesus prayed that we might be one – God's purpose and plan that we be one.

A. The Basis of This Unity.

    1. Right relationship to God.

    2. Right relationship to one another – members of one another.

    3. This makes for a bond stronger than even blood ties.

B. The First Church had this unity; it was a unity of:

    1. Faith – all believed the same thing.

    2. Love – they shared everything.

    3. Purpose – one accord.

    4. Because of this unity they had power in the world.

C. The devil uses the method of division in the church to defeat its purpose. He works through:

    1. Doctrinal differences.

    2. Temperament differences.

3. Unsympathetic judgment.

4. Censorious criticism (fault-finding).

5. Jealousy and envy due to the diversity of gifts.

D. Therefore, Paul lets us know that we must work to keep the unity.

1. The mind of Christ.

2. Baptism of Love.

The Journey – Divine Provisions

Text: I Kings 19:2–7

Introduction:

Elijah fleeing from Jezebel after he had slain all the prophets of Baal.

A. Elijah's strength had given out – physically and spiritually.

B. Christian's Life is pictured as a journey.

C. Many wrecks and dropouts.

D. The journey is too great for us to take alone.

E. Look at the obstacles.

    1. The world.

    2. Devil.

    3. Self.

    4. Sometimes people.

F. But God will help us as He did Elijah.

G. He told Elijah to arise and eat.

    1. We need Divine provisions.

    2. Elijah had to get up from where he was.

    3. He had to feed on God's provisions.

4. This is how it must be for us.

H. God had provided ample strength for us to make the journey through this year.

1. His spirit

2. His word

3. His church

I. But we have got to arise up and eat

Happiness is Trusting God – Truly Blessed

Text: Psalms 40:4, 42:5, 11

Introduction:

The thing that most of us, all of us want today is to be happy. Men spent their lives here on earth in pursuit of happiness. The tragedy is that we pursue things that we think will make us happy and many times after life obtaining them we find that we are not truly happy or blessed.

A. Blessed – means to be happy.

B. Happy

C. Content

D In a most favored position – not best condition but best condition

E. Things that give people happiness or blessedness.

    1. Money

    2. Position

    3. Influence or power

    4. Some people it takes very little to make them happy.

F. Real happiness comes from trusting God.

G. Happiness that is not based upon things or condition.

H. This happiness or blessed is based upon an initial deposit of trust in the bank of heaven – for sin.

I. No man is truly happy if he has not made this initial commitment.

J. The saved man is happy because he knows if he trust God, God will:

1. Deliver him fram his enemies – confident.

2. Fight his battles.

3. Feed him if he's hungry.

4. Help him if he is in trouble.

5. If he is sick, the Lord will heal him or affect his healing – if not, he has another building.

I Made a Vow Unto the Lord, and I Won't Take It Back

Text: Judges 11:34–35, Psalms 76:11

Introduction:

Christianity suffers today from a lack of total commitment. Too many people simply do not mean it when they say that they want to follow Jesus.

A. Jephthah's Vow

1. A vow made without due consideration of consequences.

2. He made a covenant with God. If you will, I will.

3. God kept his part of the bargain.

4. And Jephhah's kept his even though it breaks his heart.

B. Covenants we make with God.

1. At conversion we enter into a covenant.

2. Some people don't like to make a promise – some people never should.

3. But we must make periodic vows to supplement our main vow – Psalms 76:11.

4. The very fact that we will be tested for our profession makes it necessary to make a vow.

C. God does not merely encourage us to make vows but He enables us to keep them.

1. Our vow is a sign of our willingness to keep our part of the covenant.

The Old Man

Text: Ephesians 4:22, Colossians 3:9

Introduction:

The expression "old man" used but three times in the Bible. It is used to identify self – that is, that which governs our natural life, usurping in our being the place God should have. Every person born in the world is born with the "old man," self sitting on the throne of his heart.

A. A closer look at the "Old Man."

> 1. The eternal rival of God – self-will, God resisting, and God rejecting.
>
> 2. He opposes all that is good, causing us to do the evil we would not.
>
> 3. Someone said that it is the likeness in us of the devil.
>
> 4. It causes all the world's suffering – man pleasing self.
>
> 5. He gives us more trouble than all the people we will ever associate with.
>
> 6. He is corrupt – Ephesians 4:22.

B. What can be done about him?

> 1. Something must be done.
>
> 2. The Bible has but one answer, Crucifixion – Romans 6:6.

3. Salvation is crucifixion of self – putting off of the old man.

4. Two facts stand out:

    a. An accomplished fact.

    b. A co-crucifixion – I have been crucified with Christ.

C. Failure of Christians to act upon this in faith.

1. We have accepted salvation but have not consented to crucifixion.

2. We must continually say within ourselves – I am dead; I cannot please myself.

The Necessity of Spiritual Growth

Text: II Peter 3:18, I Peter 2:1–2

Introduction:

Tragic when something or someone fails to grow as it ought to. Growth is a fundamental fact of life, we look for it and expect it. This is true also in the spiritual realm.

A. Growth is dependent upon certain factors.

    1. Nourishment.

    2. Climate.

    3. Environment.

B. Nourishment.

    1. Eat the word.

    2. Prayers.

    3. Fellowship.

C. Spiritual decencies we suffer when we don't get proper nourishment.

    1. Knowledge.

    2. Peace – lack of assurance.

    3. Faith.

    4. Endurance – pray you can stay – spiritual iron.

5. Love – fellowship.

6. Cleansing

D. We must grow in grace.

1. That we might understand the deep things of God.

2. That we might be used of God to help others.

3. That we might remain happy and content in the Lord.

4. That we may not rob the church of its strength that should be used to help others.

The Sin of Ingratitude

Text: Luke 17:11–19, I Thessalonians 5:18

Introduction:

One of the most despicable traits an individual can have is to be ungrateful. Yet, among all of God's creatures, man possesses this trait in abundance.

A, He is by nature – ungrateful.

    1. We have to be taught to be thankful.

    2. Man is blinded by sin, his memory dulled, his tongue is struck dumb by sin.

    3. Even after we are saved, it is easy to become ungrateful.

    4. Ungrateful Christian is a contradiction of terms.

B. Let us look at the text.

C. These men were lepers.

    1. Lepers as a type of sin.

        a. Separating.

        b. Ugly.

        c. Incurable.

        d. Unclean.

D. They appealed to one man who was able to heal the leprosy.

E. They obeyed the command of Jesus and were healed as they went.

F, Only one returned to give thanks.

G. Our ungratefulness is demonstrated:

H. Not only in our refusal to praise God for cleansing us.

I. But our refusal to worship the Lord as He has requested. Pattern set in the New Commandment – 4th.

J. In our refusal or unwillingness to honor the lord with our substance – tithes and offerings.

K. In our dealing with one another.

    1. Merciful, forgiving, loving.

Sin – The Results of Sin

Text: Romans 3:9–10, 23, Ephesians 4:18, Isaiah 59:1–2, 12–13

Introduction:

Our thoughts this morning center upon one word – three letters. This word is the cause of all the trouble, tragedy, and heartache the world has ever known.

A. Three perspectives of sin.

    1. Nature – inclination or tendency to sin.

    2. State – man standing before God.

    3. Act – the specific deeds or doings of man are sinful.

B. What is sin – character.

    1. Disobedience – transgression.

    2. A disease of the soul.

    3. Rebellion – revolt against God, usually accompanied by stubbornness, arrogance, and pride.

C. The Effects of Sin.

    1.Separates from God.

    2. Blinds.

    3. Causes ignorance.

    4. Spiritual uncleanness.

5. A destructive force in any relationship, any group.

6. A reproach – causes shame.

7. A hindrance to spiritual development and roadblock to receiving the goodness of God.

8. Causes death – spiritual, physical, and eternal.

D. What must we do?

1. hrist is the answer.

2. His blood can wash.

3.His life can save.

Your Sins Have Witheld Good Things

Text: Jeremiah 5:25, Proverbs 14:34

Introduction:

Jeremiah speaks to God's people and lets them know that because of sin, they were missing out on many good things that they could be enjoying.

A. Good things that God's done for Israel:

    1. Their provider.

    2. Their protector.

    3. Their salvation.

B. Because of their sins, God:

    1. Held up the rain.

    2. Let other nations over-run them.

    3. Refused to deliver them when they call Him.

C. We today can miss the good things of God because of sin.

    1. The peace of God.

    2. The joy of God (David said restore.).

    3. The blessings of prayer (regard iniquity).

    4. The deep things of God and the high places.

5. Un-confessed and hidden sin can cause us not to prosper – natural and spiritual prosperity – Adam.

D. The exhortation is today, not to let sin make you miss out and lose out on the good things.

1. Close up heaven.

2. Put a lack of God's spiritual storehouse.

3. Confess and forsake your sins, and God will send the former and the latter rain.

He is Wonderful – His Name is Wonderful

Text: Isaiah 9:6

Introduction:

Isaiah's foreview of Christ lets us know that His name shall be called wonderful. In spite of the many wonders in the world today, He is the greatest wonder of all.

A. Wonders of the world today.

B. Scientific wonders.

C. Medical wonders.

D. Wonders of nature.

E. The greatest wonder of all is Christ – He is truly wonderful.

F. In his pre-existent glory.

G. In creation.

H. In incarnation.

I. In His earthly ministry.

J. In His crucifixion

K. In His resurrection.

L. In His ascension.

M. In His heavenly ministry.

N. His name is Wonderful in prayer and in service.

O. In my soul, He is Wonderful.

P. How he saved me, sanctified me, and filled me.

Q. He is wonderful in His keeping power.

R. He is wonderful in His comforting presence.

S. He can be wonderful to you if you let Him

Bishop Kenneth O. Robinson

Kenneth Ollin Robinson was born in Newark, New Jersey, on October 8, 1935, the second child of Robert and Catherine Robinson. At the age of four, after a fire destroyed their home, the Robinson family moved to Vauxhall, New Jersey, where Kenneth grew up. He attended public school in Vauxhall and graduated from Union High School in 1953. His mother and family had desires for Kenneth to attend Howard University and later go to law school.

However, God had other plans for him and at the age of sixteen, Kenneth was converted to Christ at the True Holiness Pentecostal Church in Vauxhall. Later, he become a member of the Church of God in Christ and after a few years joined Mt. Calvary Holiness Church in Staten Island, New York, under the Pastorate of Elder Archie Johnson, later to become Bishop Johnson. As a member of Mt. Calvary, he met and married Ada Bass, the youngest daughter of Elder Derby Bass. They have been married for 55 years and have been blessed with five children: Vanessa, Sharon, Kenneth Jr., Brenda, and Michael.

At the age of eighteen, while a member of Mt. Calvary Holiness Church, Kenneth was called to the gospel ministry. He had a great love for the Word of God and was an ardent student of the Bible, taking various correspondent courses to increase his understanding of the Word. In 1957, after serving in the U. S. Army, he became a member of the United Holy Church of America, Inc. under the Pastorate of Elder Derby Bass, his father-in-law, at Full Gospel Tabernacle. He heard the late Rev. Lilia A. Coleman lecture in the Northern District Convocation and later enrolled in the Lilia A. Coleman Bible Academy. Kenneth was the last student she had in her post-graduate class.

To help raise his family, Kenneth worked for the United States Postal Service for 32 years. He became the first black supervisor in Staten Island. Kenneth spent over half of his postal service career in management, including 16 ½ years as Postmaster of Cornwall-on-Hudson, New York.

Desiring to further his religious studies, Kenneth enrolled in the O. M. Kelly Bible and Religious Training Institute where he received a Bachelor of Theology degree from the New York School of Theology. In 1966 he was appointed Pastor of Holy Temple in Newburgh, New York, where he served for 12 years. In 1972 Kenneth attended the United Christian College where he received a Master of Theology degree in 1974. He began teaching at the college and continued his studies until he received a Doctor of Sacred Theology degree in 1976. Upon the death of Dr. Josephine Antley, he became the Vice-President of the United Christian College, and upon the passing of Dr. Irene Powell in 2005, Kenneth became the President of the United Christian College and Bible Institute, Northeast Extension. In 2009, he received from the Southern District of the United Christian College an honorary Doctor's degree for his work in the ministry and service to the United Holy Church of America, Inc.

Kenneth was ordained an Elder in the United Holy Church in 1966 and was active in the Eastern New York District as an evangelist and in the YPHA. As a young evangelist, he supported the District Convocation faithfully and was appointed a District Elder in 1974, a position he held for 18 years. He also served on the Board of Elder for 18 years. In 1979 Elder Robinson was appointed Pastor of the New Covenant Temple during a turbulent time in the church's history and served for 32 years.

In 1984 Elder Robinson was consecrated a Bishop in the United Holy Church of America, Inc. As a Bishop he served as Secretary of the Bishop's Council, Bishop of Publications, and Bishop and advisor to the General Education Department. He also served as Vice-President of the Virginia District Convocation in 1992. Kenneth was elected the Second Vice-President of the General Church and as President of the Northern District Convocation of the United Holy Church of America, Inc. in 1996. Upon the passing of General President, Bishop Odell McColium in 2005, Bishop Robinson became Vice-President of the General Church. He was elected in his own right in 2008.

Bishop Robinson has served in many capacities in his church for many years. He has traveled extensively throughout all of the church's districts and is well known and highly respected. One of his favorite activities is establishing new extensions of the United Christian College and Bible Institute in these areas: Bermuda, West Virginia, northern New Jersey, and the cities of Milwaukee, Wisconsin and St. Louis, Missouri and other extensions not connected to his church.

Bishop Robinson went home to be with the Lord – February 25, 2014.

ORDER COPIES OF THESE BOOKS NOW!

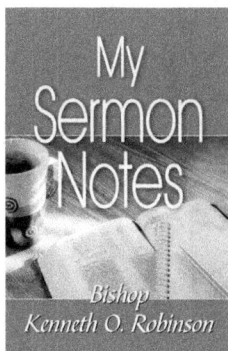

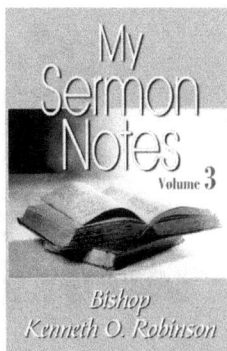

NO. OF COPIES____*My Sermon Notes* @ $20.00 each

NO. OF COPIES____*My Sermon Notes Vol. 2* @ $20.00 each

NO. OF COPIES____*My Sermon Notes Vol. 3* @ $15.00 each

_____ x no. of copies

SUBTOTAL _____

Add 6% sales tax (MD residents only) _____

Postage and handling for 1st book - $3.75 _____

P & H for each additional book - $2.00 _____

TOTAL _____

ORDERED BY _____

STREET/APT NO. _____

CITY/STATE/ZIP_____

PHONE (_____)_____

Your email address: _____
We would like to send you product updates by email.

MAKE YOUR CHECK OR MONEY ORDER TO: Ada Robinson.
PLEASE MAIL THIS ORDER FORM WITH YOUR PAYMENT TO:
DreamLife Worship Center, 4111 Deer Park Road, Randallstown, MD 21133
Please allow 2 weeks for delivery. All prices are subject to change without notice.

incahoots LITERARY presents our latest books

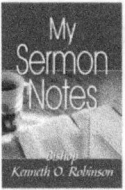

* 9 7 8 0 9 8 8 7 2 4 1 9 8 *